World Crafts and Recipes

Recipe and Craft Guide to

THE CARIBBEAN

Juliet Haines Mofford

Mitchell Lane

PUBLISHERS
P.O. Box 196
Hockessin, Delaware 19707
Visit us on the web: www.mitchelllane.com
Comments? email us: mitchelllane@mitchelllane.com

Mitchell Lane

World Crafts and Recipes

The Caribbean • China • France
India • Indonesia • Japan

PUBLISHER'S NOTE: The facts on which the story in this book is based have been thoroughly researched. Documentation of such research can be found on page 60. While every possible effort has been made to ensure accuracy, the publisher will not assume liability for damages caused by inaccuracies in the data, and makes no warranty on the accuracy of the information contained herein.

To reflect current usage, we have chosen to use the secular era designations BCE ("before the common era") and CE ("of the common era") instead of the traditional designations BC ("before Christ") and AD (*anno Domini*, "in the year of the Lord").

Library of Congress Cataloging-in-Publication
Mofford, Juliet Haines.
  Recipe and craft guide to the Caribbean / by Juliet Haines Mofford.
      p. cm. — (World crafts and recipes)
  Includes bibliographical references and index.
  ISBN 978-1-58415-935-3 (library bound)
  1. Cookery, Caribbean—Juvenile literature.
  2. Handicraft—Caribbean Area—Juvenile literature. I. Title.
  TX716.A1M654 2010
  641.59729—dc22
                                              2010009240

Printing   1   2   3   4   5   6   7   8   9
                                                    PLB

CONTENTS

Introduction: A Tropical Garden of Eden 4

Tropical Fruit Salad 10

Caribbean Coconut Rice 12

Calabash Bowl 14

Callaloo 16

A Miniature Treasure Chest 18

Haitian *Griot* 20

Seed Beads 22

Arroz con Pollo...24

Tembleque—A Christmas Pudding 26

Los Tres Reyes—Three Kings' Day 28

Musical Instruments: Maracas, Guiro 29

Steel Drums 30

Plantation Gingerbread with Lemon Sauce...32

Sew a Spice Bag 34

Make a Mask for Carnival 36

Stamp and Go, or Poor Man's Fritters..40

Make a Mobile 42

Flying Fish from Barbados 44

Sailors' Valentines—Maritime Mosaics 46

Banana Bread 48

Fly Your Own Jolly Roger 50

Jerk Chicken for a Buccaneer's Barbecue..54

A Bouquet of Tropical Flowers 56

Curried Lamb..58

Further Reading 60

   Books 60

   Works Consulted...60

   On the Internet..61

Glossary...62

Index...63

A Tropical Garden of Eden

"Always the land of the same beauty and the fields very green and full of an infinity of fruits . . . the mountains full of trees . . . and everywhere there was the perfume of flowers and the singing of birds, very sweet," Christopher Columbus wrote in his journal in 1493, on the second of four voyages through the Caribbean Islands. He wrote that he believed he was in the Garden of Eden. "I saw so many islands, I hardly knew which I would go to first."

The 2,600-mile-long archipelago that stretches from Florida to Venezuela is called the West Indies because this famous mariner believed he had found the route to India by sailing west. More than 7,000 islands form a crescent in the Caribbean Sea, of which 51 are inhabited. Others are mere islets and cays, while some are simply the tops of submerged mountains. Cuba is the largest, followed by Hispaniola, which contains Haiti and the Dominican Republic, then Jamaica and Puerto Rico, all comprising the Greater Antilles. The Lesser Antilles—from the eastern Caribbean Isles south to Trinidad and west to Aruba—are divided into the Leeward and Windward Islands. The Leewards include the British and U.S. Virgin Islands; the Windwards include Dominica and Martinique; Grenada, St. Vincent, the tiny Grenadines; and Trinidad and Tobago.

Of course Columbus wasn't the first to discover the West Indies, since the Taíno, Arawak, and Carib Indians had migrated there centuries before, from what is now South America. One can still view petroglyphs, or rock drawings, on some islands, and the indigenous peoples' legacy lives on in Caribbean cooking. The Arawaks had dugout canoes, raised corn and tobacco, made pottery, and wove cloth. They gave us the word *hamaca* or *hammock,* which says something about their lifestyle.

The Caribs preferred hunting and fishing to farming. They often raided Arawak villages, killing and eating the men and kidnapping the women for

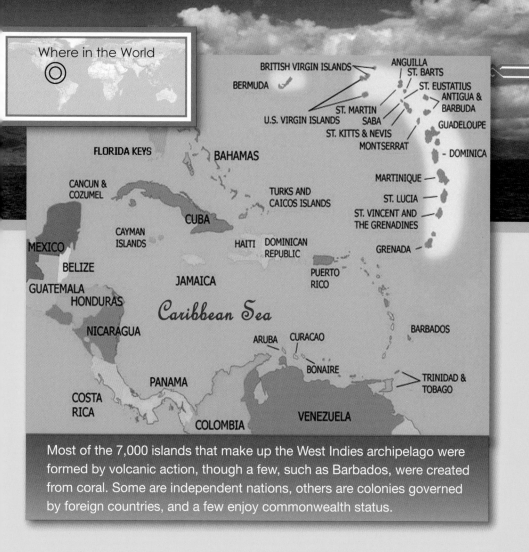

BRITISH VIRGIN ISLANDS
BERMUDA
ANGUILLA
ST. BARTS
ST. EUSTATIUS
ANTIGUA &
BARBUDA
ST. MARTIN
U.S. VIRGIN ISLANDS   SABA
ST. KITTS & NEVIS
MONTSERRAT
GUADELOUPE
– DOMINICA
FLORIDA KEYS   – BAHAMAS
CANCUN &
COZUMEL
TURKS AND
CAICOS ISLANDS
MARTINIQUE —
ST. LUCIA —
ST. VINCENT AND —
THE GRENADINES
CUBA
CAYMAN
ISLANDS
MEXICO
BELIZE
HAITI DOMINICAN
REPUBLIC
GRENADA –
GUATEMALA
HONDURAS
JAMAICA
PUERTO
RICO
Caribbean Sea
NICARAGUA
BARBADOS
ARUBA   CURACAO
BONAIRE
TRINIDAD &
TOBAGO
PANAMA
COSTA
RICA
COLOMBIA
VENEZUELA

Most of the 7,000 islands that make up the West Indies archipelago were formed by volcanic action, though a few, such as Barbados, were created from coral. Some are independent nations, others are colonies governed by foreign countries, and a few enjoy commonwealth status.

wives. The Arawaks were cruelly exploited by Europeans, especially the Spanish conquistadores in their relentless search for gold. Within several generations, the Arawaks disappeared. The Caribs, however, took on the Spanish, French, Dutch, and English, resisting colonization longer than any other tribe in the New World. Driven from island to island, their descendants remain in the mountains and rain forest of Dominica, since Great Britain and France finally agreed to let the Caribs have this island, which Columbus named "Sunday" in Spanish. Another Carib stronghold was St. Vincent. Some 2,000 Caribs living there were killed in May 1902 when Mount Soufrière erupted during the same volcanic cataclysm that killed nearly every person in Martinique's major town of St. Pierre. Only a prisoner in the dungeon and a man on the coast survived, though the latter was severely burned.

Besides volcanic eruptions, these beautiful islands of sun, sea, and surf, so favored by tourists and yachtsmen, have suffered countless natural disasters throughout history. A terrible earthquake devastated several cities on the island nation of Haiti in January 2010. Previous earthquakes, followed by tsunamis, completely destroyed Jamestown, the first capital of the island of Nevis. The sole survivor there was a pirate named Redlegs Greaves, who was locked in a dungeon, waiting to be hanged. In 1692, Port Royal, Jamaica, a favorite hangout for pirates, also suffered an earthquake and was swept away by the sea.

Hurricanes are regular seasonal occurrences throughout the West Indies. There is much lore among Caribbean sailors and fishermen regarding weather patterns. For example, they warn against sailing during any month with the letter *r* in it, for those are the worst times for hurricanes.

Each island has its own unique history. Portuguese explorers arrived in the 1400s, and a century later, Spain laid claim to the islands. By 1625, there were English and French settlements on St. Christopher (St. Kitts). Portuguese from Brazil shared their knowledge of planting and processing sugarcane with the French and English. Haiti became the world's first black republic after 1791 when African slaves revolted under the leadership of Toussaint L'Ouverture and claimed their freedom.

The Caribbean Islands became pawns in the European wars. St. Lucia changed hands between France and England fourteen times, and this history is reflected in the cuisine. One island remains half Dutch as St. Maarten, while the French half is St. Martine. And Martinique proudly bears the title Little Paris, Pearl of the Antilles.

Barbados is the only island that, once colonized, never changed hands. It has been British since 1625 when Captain John Powell claimed it for King James I. Sugar soon became the cash crop, and by 1673 there were 30,000 African slaves working its cane fields. Because of the economic success of sugar, the British counted one West Indian island worth more than all thirteen colonies in the present United States. In 1763, England nearly kept Guadeloupe and gave Canada to France.

Curaçao's architecture still resembles that of a Dutch village from the 1700s, though its economy is based on refineries that process crude oil from Venezuela. Aruba, off the northern coast of Venezuela, boasts oil refineries but is nearly as dry as a desert, while Bonaire is famous for flamingos. As well as sharing the isle of St. Martin with France, the Netherlands claimed

Saba, Suriname, and St. Eustatius (Statia). Six different national flags flew over St. Croix, St. John, and St. Thomas before 1917, when Denmark sold these Virgin Islands to the United States for $25 million. Today, nearly half of St. John is a national park.

The result of so many cultures with different histories is an amazing variety of menus. On a Dutch island, one can expect *rijstaffel,* an Indonesian rice table, and *keshi yena,* which is Edam cheese stuffed with meat, onions, tomatoes, pickles, olives, and raisins, then baked. French cuisine is typical on Martinique, Guadeloupe, and Marie Galante, with fish *blaff* a must. The fish may have been caught in the Caribbean Sea, but it arrives at the table covered with French sauces. Fried armadillo and opossum stew show up on Trinidad menus. *Tee-tee-ree,* fried cakes made of tiny fish, are a favorite in Dominica, though "mountain chicken," toads caught at night using torches, is the chief delicacy of this island, as well as of Montserrat.

Lambi, meat from the conch, is for sale nearly everywhere, strung together and slung over the shoulders of street peddlers. The conch is very stubborn about leaving its lovely pink-and-white shell, but digging it out is well worth the effort. Not only does it taste better than lobster, you also get a horn to blow!

When cooking Caribbean dishes, you'll need to observe the same rules in the kitchen as when preparing other types of food.

- Work under the supervision of an adult from start to finish.
- Read each recipe carefully and note what ingredients and special utensils are needed. Some ingredients may be easier to find and cheaper to purchase in health food stores, food co-ops, or farmer's markets than in big-chain grocery stores.
- Wash hands thoroughly each time you prepare food—before and after.
- Wash raw fruits and vegetables before preparation.
- Use a cutting board to slice vegetables.
- Wooden spoons do not conduct heat and are good choices for stirring stovetop dishes.
- Many of the recipes in this book are stir-fried, using oil for heat. If oil in a skillet should smoke or seem too hot, quickly turn off the heat. Do not move the pan or throw water in it. Allow it to cool down and begin again. Keep an open box of baking soda handy to throw on a stove fire.
- Wear oven mitts when lifting lids from hot pans, such as pans of rice. Steam from inside the pan can burn your skin.
- If you do get burned from steam or hot oil, hold the burned area of skin under cold running water. Do not apply butter.
- Clean up promptly after creating each recipe. Be sure stove dials are turned to OFF.

Lots of rice and beans are consumed on the islands, although the Cubans prefer black beans, the Puerto Ricans, red, and those whose heritage is British, pigeon peas. *Ropa vieja,* a beef stew whose name translates to "old clothes," is a favorite dish. Green bananas or plantains, which must be cooked before eaten, are as common on plates in the Dominican Republic, Puerto Rico, and Cuba as french fries are in the United States. *Tostones,* or fried plantains, seem to come with every meal on the Spanish-speaking islands.

Most Caribbean people prefer their food hot and spicy. Pepper pot is a stew that simmers on the stoves of nearly every West Indian island, whose inhabitants swear that "the longer it cooks, the better it tastes." Even the Arawaks kept a pepper pot on their fires, adding new ingredients now and then. There are plenty of sherbets and drinks made from the abundant tropical fruits to cool the palate: mango, guava, papaya, and soursop ices; coconut and avocado ice cream; even homemade ginger ale.

Foo-Foo

Many Caribbean foods were brought on slave ships from Africa and have kept their African names. *Funchi* is cornmeal mush. *Coo-coo* is a cake made of cornmeal and the African vegetable okra. *Fungee* is a dumpling made of okra, sweet potato, cornmeal, and spices. *Foo-foo* is made from boiled green plantains that are mashed, rolled into balls, and eaten with soup. The African tradition of carrying fruit, vegetables, and other burdens in big baskets atop one's head continues throughout the islands.

Nearly every plant significant to Caribbean cooking originated outside the islands. Through trade with Indonesia, the Dutch brought spices such as nutmeg and mace, cloves, ginger, and cinnamon. Sugar came from the East Indies, while cacao (to make chocolate), cassava, and arrowroot were brought from South America. Bananas arrived from the Canary Islands, and lime trees from India.

Breadfruit was brought from Tahiti to these sugar islands to plant as a cheap staple to feed slaves. Captain William Bligh was on this mission for Mother England when he lost the HMS *Bounty* to its famous mutiny and was set adrift with eighteen crew members. He finally made it back in 1793, bringing more breadfruit plants, first to St. Vincent, then to Jamaica. Breadfruit cannot be eaten right off the tree; a starchy vegetable, it is used much like a potato. A tree from one of the saplings brought by Captain Bligh to the West Indies still grows in the Botanical Gardens at Kingstown, St. Vincent.

There is no order or separation in Caribbean food servings. Fish and meat often appear on the same plate at the same time, surrounded by piles of root and green vegetables. West Indian meals are typically prepared in kitchens that are open-sided huts with thatched roofs, located away from the house where the meals are eaten.

Tropical Fruit Salad

Just pick the fruit off the trees to create this healthful Caribbean treat. Pineapples arrived in the West Indies from South America with the Carib Indians. Columbus took note of the strange, prickly fruit in his journal, for Europeans had never seen pineapples before.

Preparation Time: 25 minutes
Makes 3-4 servings
Ingredients
1 fresh pineapple
1 paw-paw (papaya)
2 ripe avocados
2 ripe mangoes
2 tablespoons mayonnaise
1 tablespoon brown sugar
Juice of ½ fresh lime
Juice of 1 orange
1½ tablespoons shredded
    coconut

Make this recipe under adult supervision.

Directions
1. Cut ¼ inch off the bottom of a pineapple. Then, using a sharp knife, cut it in half lengthwise to use as a serving bowl or boat for the salad. Cut the middle of each pineapple half into bite-sized chunks, saving the juice.
2. Peel and remove the seeds from the papaya, avocados, and mangoes, saving any juices that drip from the mangoes and adding this to the pineapple juice. Cut the avocados, papaya, and mangoes into bite-sized chunks and add them to the pineapple pieces.
3. Combine all the fruit in a large bowl with the mayonnaise, sugar, citrus juices, and juices from the pineapple and mangoes that you cut, and stir.
4. Put everything into the pineapple shell and garnish with shredded coconut.

Caribbean Coconut Rice

The West Indians like to pick coconuts from palm trees when the husk is green and the inside soft as jelly. Sold at open markets or roadside stands, *coco frio,* or coconut water, is the perfect thirst-quencher. The proprietor simply lops the top off a coconut with his machete, fashions a spoon from the husk, and offers it with a straw.

"Give me a coconut tree to shelter me from sun, rain, and wind and I need never work again!" goes the saying. Indeed, the versatility of this fruit is endless, from green coconut water through countless sweet and savory recipes to the copra that becomes the basis for soap, shampoo, hand cream, and suntan lotion.

Coco is the Portuguese or Spanish name for "ugly face" or "hobgoblin," and coconuts sold in U.S. supermarkets are actually the inside nuts that have matured into hard, oily meat. The shell makes a useful dish. To crack one open requires a hammer, causing one to wonder why monkeys find it so easy. First, cover a counter with newspaper. Then, with the permission of **an adult,** use a hammer and nail to puncture three eyes. Drain the milk into a bowl. Break the coconut into pieces with the hammer and remove the meat. Scrape off the brown skin with a vegetable peeler. If you bake the open coconut at 300°F for ten minutes, the meat will separate from the shell easier. Grate the meat and pour two cups of boiling water over it. Let this stand 15 minutes. Then stir, drain, and press through a sieve several times to squeeze out the milk. Use immediately, since coconut milk only lasts overnight in the refrigerator

Preparation time: 15 minutes
Makes 2-4 servings

Ingredients

2	teaspoons butter
2	teaspoons minced fresh ginger
1	clove garlic, minced
1	cinnamon stick
1	cup rice (jasmine rice works well)
¾	cup coconut milk
1	teaspoon sugar
½	teaspoon salt
¼	teaspoon grated lime zest
⅛	teaspoon white pepper
¼	cup toasted shredded coconut

Make this recipe under adult supervision.

Directions
1. In a saucepan, melt the butter over medium heat.
2. Add the ginger, garlic, and cinnamon stick. Sauté 1 minute, or until you can smell the spices.
3. Stir in the rice and sauté 2 minutes.
4. Add coconut milk, sugar, salt, lime zest, white pepper, and ¾ cup water. When it starts to simmer, stir it once, cover, and reduce heat to low. Let it simmer for 15 minutes.
5. Fluff the rice with a fork and put the lid back on. Let it sit for 5 minutes.
6. Sprinkle toasted coconut on top and serve.

Calabash Bowl

The useful calabash or bottle gourd was one of the first plants in the world to be cultivated, perhaps because it has so many uses. It arrived in the Caribbean from Africa on slave ships. These pale green balls can be cooked as a vegetable when harvested mature, hollowed out to be used as bowls, spoons, bottles, pipes, and even musical instruments. Dried calabashes make handy canteens for carrying water. Strung on a rope, they can be used as shoulder packs for fishermen's bait or the day's catch. Calabashes are painted and decorated by island artisans and sold at markets and tourist shops.

You'll Need:

- Old newspapers and blank newsprint
- A shallow pan for the papier-mâche solution
- White flour
- White glue
- Warm water
- A plastic bowl for the mold (such as one used for instant noodles)
- Petroleum jelly
- Scissors
- Pencil and paper
- Acrylic or poster paints
- Paintbrushes
- Acrylic varnish

Directions

1. Tear old newspapers and blank newsprint into strips 4 inches long and 1½ inches wide. Rip newspapers from the fold down.
2. Stir ½ cup flour into ½ cup of warm water and ½ cup of white glue. The solution should have the consistency of heavy cream. If it seems too thick, add more warm water.
3. Cover the inside of the bowl lightly with petroleum jelly. Turn the bowl upside down and cover the outside.

4. Pull strips of the torn paper through the papier-mâche solution one piece at a time. Drain off any excess by holding each strip up and pulling it between your fingers before laying it on the mold.
5. Lay the strips one at a time across, around, and inside the bowl, placing each one in the opposite direction from the previous strip until there are 5 layers. To make painting easier later, apply blank newsprint as the final layer. If the project seems too wet, alternate the layers with dry strips.
6. Let the bowl dry upside-down overnight.
7. Remove the plastic dish that served as your mold. Then, with the scissors, trim the top edges even, clipping off any loose pieces of newspaper.
8. Paint your bowl inside and out using a solid color. Let it dry and add another coat of the same color. Dry it overnight again.
9. Sketch out designs on paper. Then decorate your bowl.
10. When the bowl is dry, coat it inside and out with a layer of varnish.

Callaloo

Hearty soups filled with a variety of green and root vegetables, meat, shellfish, and spices represent a staple of the West Indian diet. Every island has its own favorite and manner of cooking these one-pot meals. Callaloo is popular throughout the Caribbean but it is prepared differently on each island, if not in every household. There isn't even agreement on spelling: whether it begins with *C* or *K* or contains one or two *Ls*. Its heritage is African, where it took its name from the leaves of the dasheen, taro, or eddo plant that resembles green elephant ears. Since this root vegetable is seldom available in the United States, kale or spinach can be substituted. Okra is also of African origin, and though its fuzzy outside and gooey inside might not please all palates, it is a familiar ingredient in Creole recipes such as gumbo. Cooks on the Dutch Islands make callaloo with pigs' tails, while those of St. Vincent prefer salted beef; on Martinique and Guadeloupe, salt pork is preferred, with crabmeat. Ham hocks are tossed into the pots of Jamaica and Trinidad, along with shrimp.

Preparation Time: 20 Minutes
Cooking Time: 30 minutes
Ingredients

1   pound kale or spinach
1   medium onion, chopped
2   scallions or green onions, chopped
1   green pepper, chopped
1   garlic clove, chopped
½   teaspoon chili pepper or 1 small Scotch bonnet, seeds removed and chopped (optional)
½   cup chopped celery
2   tablespoons butter
4   cups of chicken broth
¾   cup cooked ham, cut into cubes
8   okras (or sugar snap peas), cut into ½-inch pieces

½   cup unsweetened coconut milk (available at most supermarkets, Asian or West Indian stores)
1   whole clove or ½ teaspoon ground cloves
½   teaspoon allspice
¼   teaspoon coriander
½   teaspoon salt
¼   teaspoon pepper
1   pound or one can of crabmeat, drained (or 8 medium fresh shrimp)
½   teaspoon dried thyme

Make this recipe under adult supervision.

Directions

1. Wash kale or spinach thoroughly and cut into 2-inch pieces, discarding stems.
2. Sauté onion, scallions, green pepper, garlic, chili pepper, and celery in butter for 5 minutes, stirring to keep from browning.
3. Add broth and ham and bring to a boil.
4. Add kale or spinach, the okra or sugar snap peas, coconut milk, cloves, allspice, coriander, salt, and pepper. Reduce heat and cook slowly, uncovered, about 12 minutes.
5. Flake crabmeat and put in pot with dried thyme. Cook 5 minutes more (or cook the cleaned shrimp in ¼ cup water about 5 minutes, then add to the pot and simmer on low heat for another 15 minutes).

A Miniature Treasure Chest

Shells of many shapes, sizes, and colors can be found on beaches throughout the West Indies. Jewelry, boxes, and other crafts made of shells by local artisans are for sale on every Caribbean island. For this project, you can find unpainted wooden boxes of different sizes at craft stores. You may not live or vacation near a beach, but you can still find bags of shells at crafts stores or online. If you gather your own shells at the beach, soak them in vinegar or a mixture of ¼ cup bleach and a gallon of water, so they will be thoroughly clean before use.

You'll Need:

- An unpainted wooden box (or a plain cardboard box)
- A piece of fine-grain sandpaper
- Old newspapers or a plastic sheet
- Tempera or acrylic paints
- Paintbrush
- A variety of small shells
- A ruler
- Pencil and paper
- White glue
- Small paintbrush for applying glue
- Stickers or pictures (optional)
- A piece of felt or other fabric, or pictures cut from magazines and varnish

Directions

1. If your box has any rough edges, rub them smooth with sandpaper.
2. Cover your work surface with newspapers or a plastic sheet. Paint the outside of the box with 3 or 4 coats, letting the paint dry thoroughly between each coat.
3. Lay out the shells you plan to use on a table and, following the dimensions of your box, create a pattern with the shells, organizing them by color, shape, and size. Sketch your design with pencil and paper. Decide whether to paint the inside of your box, cover it with pictures, or keep it plain and simple.
4. Following your design, apply glue with a brush onto the back of a shell and press it onto the box. Add the other shells the same way, one at a time. Be careful not to get glue on the hinges or clasp.
5. If you do not plan to paste pictures inside your box, cut a piece of felt or fabric the same size as the bottom of the inside of your box and glue it inside. If you use pictures, be sure to cover them later with a layer of protective varnish.

Haitian *Griot*

Griot, or marinated pork, is considered Haiti's national dish. It is enjoyed there both as a main meal and as a snack. Haitians like it made with fiery hot peppers, but you can eliminate the peppers if you want.

Preparation Time: 15 minutes; marinate 2 hours
Cooking Time: 40 minutes

Ingredients

1-2 pounds pork loin, without fat and cut into bite-sized cubes
1 medium onion, diced
2 scallions, chopped
½ teaspoon powdered chili pepper or 1 Scotch bonnet pepper, seeds removed and chopped (optional)
1 green pepper, chopped
2 cloves garlic, minced
½ cup fresh lime juice
½ cup fresh orange juice
¼ cup water
½ teaspoon dried thyme
¼ teaspoon salt
¼ teaspoon black pepper
2 tablespoons light olive oil
Rice cooked according to package directions (if desired)

Make this recipe under adult supervision.

Directions
1. Cut up the pork and place it in a bowl. Add all the other ingredients except the olive oil. Marinate in the refrigerator for 2 hours or more.
2. Drain the meat, saving the marinade in another bowl.
3. Heat the olive oil in a pan. Add the meat and brown it on all sides.
4. Add the marinade with the vegetables and citrus juices. Cover and simmer over low heat 30 minutes.
5. Remove the cover and simmer another 10 minutes until the pork is tender and most of the liquid is absorbed. Serve hot over rice.

Seed Beads

Like calabash dishes, baskets, shell jewelry, and woven mats, beads made of seeds common in the West Indies are cottage-industry items, made at home to be sold to tourists or peddled from door to door. Since one cannot find Job's tears or red-and-black jumbie beads in the United States, you can make a necklace from found objects and clay.

You'll Need:

- Clay of different colors
- Toothpicks
- Wrapping paper or wallpaper
- Glue
- Pencil
- Plastic straws and/or uncooked macaroni or ziti
- Watermelon seeds (optional)
- A large needle, such as an embroidery needle
- Scissors
- Thin, strong string or plastic ribbon

Directions

1. Before making your beads, think about what you wish to make, including the various colors, sizes, and shapes of the beads. Consider different arrangements.
2. Roll small pieces of clay around with your fingers to create cubes, balls, ovals, teardrops, and tubes.
3. When you finish forming each bead, use a toothpick to poke a hole through it large enough for stringing. With **an adult's help,** bake the clay (or not) according to package directions.
4. You can also make tube-shaped beads using wrapping paper or wallpaper. Select the prettiest designs and cut them into 1-inch strips. Spread glue over each strip of paper and roll it tightly around a pencil. Then carefully pull the pencil out. Allow the "beads" to dry overnight. Or save the seeds from a watermelon and spread them out to dry. Using an embroidery

needle, poke holes through each watermelon seed, large enough to string.

5. Cut plastic straws into 1- or 2-inch pieces to use between the fancier beads. Uncooked macaroni or ziti pieces also make good spacers.

6. Cut a piece of string long enough to fit easily over your head.

7. Tie a knot at one end of your string or yarn. Be sure the knot is larger than the holes you made in your clay shapes. String your necklace. Tie the ends together when you finish.

Arroz con Pollo

Puerto Ricans are U.S. citizens, yet most residents of this commonwealth, along with those of the independent nations of Cuba and the Dominican Republic, remain loyal to their Spanish heritage in food choices. Arroz con pollo (rice with chicken) is often on the menu.

Preparation Time: 30 minutes
Cooking Time: 30 minutes

Ingredients

2–2½ pounds chicken pieces, skinned
2 cloves garlic, minced
Juice of half a lemon
¼ teaspoon chili pepper
¼ teaspoon dried oregano
¼ teaspoon dried basil
2 tablespoons olive oil
4 cups chicken broth
8 ounces tomato sauce (or ¼ cup tomato paste)
8 ounces canned tomatoes
1 onion, chopped
1 green pepper, chopped
1 tablespoon fresh parsley
4 fresh mushrooms, sliced

¾ cup fresh or frozen peas
1 tablespoon vinegar
½ teaspoon salt
½ teaspoon black pepper
¼ teaspoon dried cumin
¼ teaspoon dried coriander
2 cups rice (uncooked—do not use instant rice)
2 cups boiling water
1 tablespoon capers
¼ cup black olives (without pits), sliced
Green and red pepper, sliced

Make this recipe under adult supervision.

Directions

1. Rub chicken with garlic, lemon juice, chili pepper, oregano, and basil.
2. Heat olive oil in a pot over medium heat. Add chicken; brown for 5 minutes on each side.
3. Remove chicken from pot and place on a plate lined with paper towels. Set aside.
4. Add chicken broth, tomato sauce, canned tomatoes, chopped onion, green peppers, parsley, mushrooms, peas, vinegar, salt, pepper, cumin, and coriander. Simmer 10 minutes.
5. Put chicken pieces back in pot. Add rice, and cover with water 1 inch higher than the rice. Boil for 3 minutes. Reduce heat and cover the pot. Cook on low heat half an hour or until chicken is tender and the rice is cooked.
6. Serve in a casserole dish. Garnish with capers, olives, and strips of red and green pepper.

Tembleque—
A Christmas Pudding

This coconut pudding, whose name means "trembling," is a must during the Christmas season on Spanish-speaking islands. Meanwhile, residents of the British Islands enjoy their own traditional seasonal pudding called sweet potato pone.

Preparation Time: 10 minutes
Cooking Time: 15 minutes
Refrigerate: 2 hours

Ingredients
½ cup cornstarch or arrowroot
1 cup regular milk
¾ cup cream of coconut (available in supermarkets, often in the international section)
3 tablespoons sugar (omit sugar if using presweetened cream of coconut)
¼ teaspoon salt
1 teaspoon vanilla
1 teaspoon ground cinnamon
Shredded coconut

Make this recipe under adult supervision.

Directions
1. In a pan, whisk cornstarch into milk. Then add the cream of coconut and sugar (unless it is presweetened) and salt. Mix well.
2. Put the pan on medium heat, stirring constantly with a wooden spoon until the mixture starts to thicken.
3. Stir in vanilla.
4. Pour into individual dessert dishes.
5. Allow the pudding to cool on a wire rack; then refrigerate several hours before serving.
6. Sprinkle cinnamon on top and garnish with shredded coconut.

For a more authentic presentation, use coconut shells instead of dessert dishes. Line the coconut shell with foil, plastic wrap, or wax paper, then sprinkle each serving with cinnamon and shredded fresh coconut.

Los Tres Reyes— Three Kings' Day

Children in the Spanish West Indies expect to receive presents on Three Kings' Day rather than Christmas morning. This holiday celebrates Twelfth Night when the Three Wise Men arrived with gifts for the newborn Jesus. Before going to sleep on January 5, the children place hay beneath their beds to feed the donkeys or camels on which the Wise Men rode to Bethlehem. Strolling musicians, strumming guitars and shaking maracas, go door to door, begging for food in exchange for singing carols to a calypso beat. *Pasteles,* made of meat, olives, vegetables, and cornmeal, then wrapped in plantain leaves and boiled, are traditionally provided. Called "scrubbing" in the British Caribbean, it's Christmas trick-or-treat.

Making Musical Instruments

Like their African and Spanish forebears, the Caribbean people make musical instruments out of gourds that grow on vines and trees. The unique sounds made by these brightly decorated musical instruments are most prevalent during Christmas and Carnival, when in Puerto Rico, *guiros* are scratched and seed-filled gourds, or maracas, are shaken. *Guiros,* which originated with Taíno Indians, are long, hollow gourds that are notched, then rubbed up and down with prongs to create haunting, rasping sounds. Wooden sticks called *palillos* are tapped together to keep the beat. Castanets, often made of clamshells, add to festive rhythms.

Maracas

You can make maracas using real gourds. These are available at supermarkets and outdoor stands during the fall harvest season. Use them for decoration for a month (say, through Thanksgiving), then paint them with West Indian designs and shake them.

Guiros

On all the Spanish and some British islands, *guiros* are used with maracas by traveling troubadours, especially at Christmastime. Find a long, narrow gourd and let it dry for several weeks. Ask **an adult** to use a knife to make parallel grooves down one side of the gourd. Using a wooden stick or metal prong, rub up and down over the grooves to capture a traditional, rhythmic Caribbean beat.

Catch That Calypso Beat
Steel Drums

Another festive instrument is the steel drum, which originated in Trinidad and Tobago during World War II. Made of oil drums that have been indented to create musical notes, steel drums have become the most familiar sound of the West Indies, a sound you can imitate using an old coffee can.

You'll Need:

- An empty metal can with no rough edges, the bigger the better (a family-sized coffee can will do nicely)
- Permanent marker with a medium tip
- Acrylic paints
- Paintbrush
- A quarter or bottle cap about the size of a quarter
- Small hammer
- Pair of small wooden drumsticks

Directions

1. Remove all labels on the can, then paint it a solid dark color.
2. Turn the can upside down. Trace around a quarter or bottle top with a permanent marker to make five circles on top, one in each quarter of the lid and the fifth circle in the middle.
3. Using a small hammer, carefully pound shallow dents on four of these circles, leaving one untouched. With each circle dented to a different depth and one circle undented, you can create a variety of notes.
4. Use small wooden drumsticks, or even a pencil, to capture your own Caribbean sounds.

Plantation Gingerbread
with Lemon Sauce

Sugarcane was introduced from Brazil to Barbados in the 1630s, sparking the Triangle Trade. Thousands of people were kidnapped, shipped from their homes in Africa, and sold as slaves in the Caribbean. They labored in cane fields, and were forced to process the cane into sugar, molasses, and rum. These products were traded at Atlantic seaports for lumber, cattle, textiles, wheat, and salt cod.

Only a few islands such as Dominica and St. Vincent, dominated by Carib Indians, escaped the abuses brought by the sugarcane industry. Plantations varied in size, and masters varied in treatment of slaves. Raising cane required a large, cheap labor force working from dawn to dusk. Between 1700 and 1774, half a million slaves were transported to Jamaica alone.

This recipe includes products obtained from sugarcane, mixed with Caribbean spices.

Preparation Time: 30 minutes
Cooking Time: 45 minutes
Make this recipe under adult supervision.

Ingredients

2 eggs	1¼ teaspoon cinnamon
¾ cup (1½ sticks) melted butter	½ teaspoon ground cloves
	½ teaspoon ground nutmeg
1 cup brown sugar	½ teaspoon salt
1 cup molasses	2 teaspoons baking powder
2½ cups flour	½ teaspoon baking soda
1¼ teaspoon ginger	1 cup boiling water

Directions

1. Heat oven to 350°F.
2. Beat eggs lightly.
3. Combine butter or oil with brown sugar, molasses, and beaten eggs. Mix until fluffy.
4. Add flour, spices, and baking powder and mix thoroughly.
5. Combine baking soda with boiling water and add to batter.
6. Pour batter into a buttered pan and bake for 35 minutes or until a toothpick poked in the middle comes out clean. Meanwhile, make Lemon Sauce (below).
7. While the gingerbread is still warm, poke a few holes in it with a fork and pour the lemon sauce over it.

Lemon Sauce

½   cup sugar
2   tablespoons cornstarch
1   cup water
2   egg yolks
½   cup (1 stick) butter, sliced
   Juice from one lemon
   Grated lemon peel

Directions

1. Mix sugar and cornstarch.
2. Heat the water over low heat in a medium-size pan. Using a wire whisk, gradually stir in the sugar and cornstarch mixture until it thickens.
3. Beat egg yolks lightly. While stirring the liquid in the pan, add the yolks. Continue to stir for a few minutes so that the eggs don't harden.
4. Remove the pan from the heat. Add butter and stir until it is melted. Then add lemon juice and peel, and stir.

Sew a Spice Bag

Columbus may not have found all the spices he was seeking on his voyages to the islands he mistakenly called the Indies, but the islands now offer a treasure trove of exotic flavors. Grenada is called "The Spice Island," with more spices per square mile than any other place in the world. Columbus never set foot on Grenada, although he sighted it on his third voyage. The Caribs drove him away, as they did the Englishmen who attempted to land there in 1609. The French settled Grenada in 1650 by trading knives and liquor with the Caribs, who soon attempted to reclaim the island. When trapped by French musketfire, most Caribs jumped into the sea rather than surrender.

Grenada has developed a thriving cottage industry of spices, supplying the world through mail-order catalogs. One can even get hand-rolled balls of cacao (cocoa), which can be processed into chocolate, and fresh vanilla beans. Planted by British colonists around 1840, nutmeg trees bear fruit resembling fresh apricots. Inside, wound in webs of scarlet mace, hide the nutmegs.

To spice your home with the fragrances of the islands, you can make a bag and fill it with tropical spices like nutmeg, cloves, and cinnamon. Add dried orange peel, and this spice bag will be useful not only in the kitchen, but as a natural air freshener for your closet.

You'll Need:

- A piece of cotton fabric, about 12 by 18 inches
- Straight pins
- Scissors
- Needle
- Thread to match the fabric
- Measuring tape
- Ribbon or string, 1 foot long
- A medium-sized safety pin
- Cloves, whole or powdered
- Cinnamon sticks
- Nutmegs, broken in half
- Vanilla beans
- Dried orange or lemon peels (lay fresh peels on a windowsill in the sun until they are curled)
- Powdered allspice in a small sandwich bag (optional)

Directions

1. Fold the fabric in half crosswise. Using straight pins, pin the sides together.

2. Use scissors to round the corners on the fold, but leave most of the fold in place.

3. Remove the pins and turn the material inside out. Pin the sides again.

4. Sew the sides of the bag together. Be sure to leave the top open.

5. Fold the top of the bag down about an inch and pin it. This is where the drawstring will go. Holding the bag open with one hand, sew around the bottom edge of the fold. Be careful not to sew the bag closed.

6. Now turn the bag right side out. Using a safety pin to anchor the drawstring, feed one end all the way through the 1-inch space at the top. Be sure the other end still hangs out the other side. Knot the ends or sew them together.

7. Fill your spice bag with cloves, cinnamon sticks, nutmegs, vanilla beans, and pieces of dried orange or lemon peel. Ground allspice is powdery, so if you use it, put it in a small plastic bag inside the spice bag.

Make a Mask for Carnival

The biggest celebration every year is Carnival, when residents and visitors make merry for several days, sometimes the whole week, just before the solemn Catholic season of Lent. The more colorful the costumes, the more outrageous the calypso lyrics, the louder the steel drums, the more everyone enjoys *Mas.*

During Carnival throughout the islands, festival kings and queens are elected, and prizes are awarded for costumes. Some are so huge and heavy that wheels are required to carry those wearing them through the crowded streets. The star of the show is usually Moko Jumby, the witch doctor of African folklore, who walks on stilts.

A Mask for Carnival

Only a few people walk on stilts, but nearly everyone, including small children, wears costumes and masks, the sillier or scarier the better. In Puerto Rico, *vejigante* masks are traditionally carved from coconut husks, with sharp teeth and horns to fend off evil. People who wear them, also called *vejigantes*, are tricksters. They play harmless pranks on people during the last Sunday of Carnival.

You'll Need:

- White flour or white glue
- Warm water
- Bucket or flat pan
- Old newspapers
- Plain newsprint
- A large, round balloon
- Large bowl or empty can (to use for a stand)
- Scissors
- Tubes from toilet paper rolls or cardboard from egg cartons (optional)
- Masking tape
- Tempera paints
- Paintbrushes
- Feathers, stickers, yarn, or other decorations
- String

Directions

1. Mix 1 part flour with 1 part warm water (or white liquid glue with water) for papier-mâche solution.
2. Tear newspapers and newsprint in strips 1½ inches wide.
3. Blow up and knot a round balloon bigger than your head.
4. Pull strips of newspaper through papier-mâche solution, one at a time, squeezing out any excess between your fingers. Cover the balloon with at least five layers, alternating them horizontally and vertically. Press layers to remove air pockets, lumps, or excess water. Finish with a layer of plain newsprint for easier painting.
5. Place the project on an empty can or large bowl. Let it dry.

6. When thoroughly dry, cut the sphere in half to make two separate masks. Hold one half up to your face to determine where the eyes, nose, and mouth should be. With the help of **an adult,** cut holes for these.
7. Cut cardboard tubes or the bottom of egg cartons if you wish to add a long nose, horns, big ears, or sharp teeth. Attach these to the mask with masking tape, securing them with several more layers of papier-mâché. Allow the mask to dry overnight again.
8. Paint the whole mask and let it dry. Decorate it with polka dots and stripes if you wish. Use glue to add feathers, yarn, or felt.
9. Punch a hole on each side of the mask just above your ears. Thread a piece of string through each hole so that you can tie your mask on.

Stamp and Go, or Poor Man's Fritters

Stamp and Go has been popular since the days of slavery. Although the sea surrounding the West Indies is abundant with delicious varieties of fish, Europeans who managed the sugar plantations preferred to feed their slaves cheap, salt codfish imported from New England. The recipe has been passed down through generations and remains common throughout the Caribbean Islands. These cakes, made from dry, salted cod, are known as *bacalaitos* in the Spanish islands, *accras de morue* on French islands, and "poor man's fritters" elsewhere. No one knows why Jamaicans call them Stamp and Go, but supposedly, when the people residing on that large island crave one, they simply jump off their donkeys or hop off the bus and pick up a codfish cake from a roadside stand. It is especially popular for breakfast in Jamaica, where it is eaten with ackee, a golden fruit that grows there in abundance but is difficult to find on the other islands.

In the United States, dried salt cod is sold at most fish stores. It comes from Newfoundland, already cleaned and boned, and packed in a wooden box.

Preparation Time: Soak overnight; then 25 minutes
Cooking Time: 15 minutes

Ingredients

1	pound dried salt cod, boned
½	cup cooking oil
1	large onion, chopped
2	green onions or scallions, chopped
½	green pepper, chopped
½	red pepper, chopped
2	cloves garlic, pressed
2	cups flour
2	teaspoons baking powder
1	teaspoon chili powder, or ½ Scotch bonnet hot pepper, seeds removed and chopped (optional)
½	teaspoon black pepper
1	teaspoon thyme
1	tablespoon parsley flakes or 2 sprigs of fresh parsley, chopped
1	egg, lightly beaten
1	cup milk

Make this recipe under adult supervision.

Directions

1. Cut salt cod into pieces. Place them in a bowl and cover them with cold water. Soak overnight in the refrigerator.
2. Drain the cod, discarding the water. Rinse the cod under cold water. Even if using deboned cod, check to be sure the bones are all removed. Break it into pieces and place them in a saucepan. Cover the fish with cold water again.
3. Bring the saucepan to a boil. Reduce heat to low and simmer for 15 minutes, uncovered.
4. Have **an adult** help you rinse the hot fish under cold, running water again. Drain and set aside.
5. Heat oil in a heavy skillet. Add onion, scallions, green and red pepper, and garlic. Sauté 5 minutes.
6. Mix flour and baking powder, chili powder, and other spices together in large bowl. Add the beaten egg and milk. Stir just enough to blend ingredients. (To make this the New England way—see below—add mashed potatoes in this step.)
7. Pour ½ inch cooking oil into large frying pan and heat. Spoon batter one heaping tablespoon at a time into hot oil. Fry about 5 minutes on each side, until cakes turn brown and crisp.
8. Remove codfish cakes from pan and drain on paper towels. Serve them hot.

This recipe makes about 24 cakes, each one the size of a medium hamburger, so any left over can be wrapped and put into the freezer after they cool, for a later meal.

Salt cod cakes were also popular in Colonial New England, where mashed potatoes were used instead of some of the flour. If you'd like, substitute 2 cups flour with 1 cup flour and 1½ cups mashed potatoes (from 4 medium potatoes).

Make a Mobile

Between the Caribbean islands and the coast of Central America lie thousands of square miles of coral reefs. Besides attracting tourists for fishing and diving, the reefs are home to a wide variety of sea life, from tiny zooxanthellae to migrating sea turtles. You can make a colorful mobile to remind you of all the creatures that live among the corals.

You'll Need:

- Pencil and paper
- Pictures of sea life drawn, cut from old magazines, or printed from the Internet
- Scissors
- Tempera paints or markers
- Paintbrushes
- Cardboard
- Colored paper
- Glue
- Aluminum foil
- Stapler
- Thread
- Hole punch
- A hook

Directions

1. Draw or cut out 7 pictures of fish or other marine life, each approximately 8 x 11 inches.
2. Mount each one on colored paper.
3. Paint them in various bright colors and cut them out.
4. Decorate your marine life with glitter, or staple on pieces of aluminum foil.
5. Cut 2 or 3 pieces of cardboard one inch wide and 12 inches long. Wrap them in aluminum foil and staple them crosswise at the center.
6. Punch a hole at the top middle of each sea creature and put different lengths of string through the holes.

7. Tie them one at a time so that they all hang from the cardboard at different distances from the center. Take care to keep their threads from tangling.
8. Staple a piece of string to the middle of the cardboard hanger, and loop the string around a hook in the doorway.

Flying Fish from Barbados

Although this favorite from the easternmost Caribbean island has no wings, its extended pectoral fins allow it to leap out of the water and appear to fly. By swimming fast, these fish build up speed, then break the surface and glide at up to 40 miles per hour above the water. When the surf explodes with silver flashes, fishermen toss up their nets to capture them.

You can make this flying fish recipe using any white fish.

Preparation Time: 15 minutes;
marinate 2 hours
Cooking Time: 15 minutes

Ingredients

1 pound white fish, such as brook trout, whiting or hake, bones removed
2 cloves garlic, grated
¼ teaspoon dried thyme
1 teaspoon dried marjoram
Salt and pepper to taste
Juice of 2 limes
½ cup water
1 onion, chopped fine
2 scallions, chopped fine
1 green pepper, chopped
¾ cup flour
2 tablespoons cornmeal
½ tablespoon baking powder
1 egg, beaten
3 tablespoons milk
1 tablespoon butter or 2 tablespoons oil for frying
Lime slices

Make this recipe under adult supervision.

Directions
1. Press garlic, thyme, marjoram, salt, and pepper into the fish's flesh. Marinate in a bowl with the lime juice and water 2 hours or more.
2. Sauté onion, scallions, and green pepper, stirring 5 to 8 minutes.
3. Combine flour, cornmeal, and baking powder in a bowl.
4. In another bowl, break and beat the egg, then add the milk.
5. Remove the fish from the dish where it has been marinating. Pat it dry with paper towels.
6. Roll the fish in flour, cornmeal, and baking powder mixture, coating it thoroughly.
7. Dip fish in egg and milk mixture, one piece at a time.
8. Fry fish in cooking oil or melted butter 5 minutes on each side or until fish turns light brown.
9. Drain on paper towels and serve with onion, scallions, and green pepper. Garnish with lime slices and serve with rice and pigeon peas.
10. If you wish more lime flavor, heat the sauce used for marinating the fish. Add the leftover egg and sautéed vegetables, plus 1 tablespoon sugar and ½ tablespoon Japanese soy sauce. Pour this over the fish and rice.

Sailors' Valentines —Maritime Mosaics

Collecting, classifying, and crafting shells were favorite pastimes during the Victorian era. American ship captains and sailors, long separated from their mothers, wives, and sweethearts, liked to bring home souvenirs from their trading and whaling voyages. As the easternmost Caribbean island, Barbados was usually their last port of call, and this was where many mariners picked up gifts crafted from shells by native artisans.

Sailors' Valentines were popular keepsakes. Mothers and sweethearts, waiting so long at home, treasured these unique gifts of shells set in intricate patterns that framed their mirrors and pictures. Though not necessarily meant as gifts for Valentine's Day, they were treasured as messages of love. Flowers, fish, hearts, ships, and anchors were popular motifs, along with mermaids, those mythical maidens who sat upon reefs combing their hair to lure sailors to shipwrecks. You can create your own nautical mosaic with shells, pebbles, and beach glass. If you want to use shells you've collected from the beach, wash them well and soak them overnight in vinegar or ¼ cup bleach and a gallon of water.

You'll Need:

- Pencil and paper
- A ruler
- White glue (or double-sided foam tape)
- A brush for applying glue
- A precut wooden backing, available at crafts outlets
- Shells of various types, colors, and sizes
- Beach glass and pebbles of different shapes and colors
- Rubber stamps with maritime subjects (optional)
- Yarn (optional)
- Toothpick

Directions

1. Decide on a theme and design, and sketch it on paper. Consider the size and color of the shells, beach glass, and other materials you plan to use. A ruler can help you make sure everything will fit the way you want it to.
2. Following your design, glue the shells, pebbles and beach glass, one by one, on the wooden frame.
3. Let the project dry overnight. Then, using white glue applied with a toothpick, add yarn or other decorations as you wish.

Banana Bread

The biggest day of the week on most Caribbean islands is the day the banana boats are loaded to transport this "green gold" to Europe, Canada, and the United States. The bananas cannot be harvested until the ships anchor in port, since only 36 hours can elapse between the time the stems are cut and the bananas are loaded into the refrigerator of the ship. Since big bunches of bananas ripen all at once, West Indians have come up with countless recipes to use them—whether baked, fried, added to casseroles, or made into scrumptious cakes and breads. This banana bread calls for spices and lemons that grow in the West Indies and tastes delicious warm or cold.

Preparation Time: 20 minutes
Cooking Time: 40 minutes

Ingredients

½ cup butter
¾ cup brown sugar
2 large, ripe bananas
2 eggs, beaten
1 teaspoon vanilla extract
2½ cups flour
1 tablespoon baking powder
½ teaspoon baking soda

½ teaspoon cinnamon
¼ teaspoon ground nutmeg
¼ teaspoon ground cloves
¼ teaspoon salt
Juice of ½ fresh lemon
½ cup milk
Walnuts or pecans (optional)

Make this recipe under adult supervision.

Directions

1. Preheat oven to 350°F.
2. Butter bottom and sides of a 9-x-5-inch loaf pan, then set aside.
3. In a large bowl, cream the butter and brown sugar until light and fluffy.
4. In another bowl, mash the peeled bananas. Add beaten egg and vanilla to the bananas and mix well.
5. Sift flour, baking powder, baking soda, cinnamon, nutmeg, cloves, and salt into the larger bowl. Stir it all into the butter and sugar. Add the banana mixture.
6. Mix the milk and lemon juice in a measuring cup, then add them to the batter.
7. Beat the batter until well blended. If desired, stir in walnuts or pecans.
8. Pour the batter into the buttered loaf pan. Bake about an hour or until a toothpick inserted in the middle comes out clean. (If it browns too quickly on top, cover with a tent of aluminum foil.)
9. Allow bread to cool 10-15 minutes before removing it from the pan.

Fly Your Own Jolly Roger

With so many islands situated close together and hidden bays to lurk behind, the Caribbean was a pirate's paradise. Using smaller ships outfitted for maximum speed, buccaneers roamed the Spanish Main from 1600 through the 1780s. First encouraged by kings and merchants from England, the Netherlands, and France, pirates attacked Spanish ships loaded with gold and silver from Central and South America. They eventually recognized no national government and profited from European wars. Tortuga, among the British Virgin Islands, was their headquarters, and in spite of artists and storytellers such as Howard Pyle and Robert Louis Stevenson, pirates were more likely to spend their treasure at Port Royal in Jamaica than to bury it.

After the British captured Jamaica in 1655, the English government, fearing Spanish invasion, offered this island as a safe haven for pirates. There is no documentation that their enemies were forced to walk the plank, and pirates who survived raids against other ships and escaped hanging usually retired to run their own sugar plantations.

Representing many different nations, pirate crews generally consisted of political prisoners "Barbadoed" from Europe to the New World, sailors who had deserted national navies or had been shipwrecked, and indentured servants and slaves escaping cruel masters. They lived by a democratic code, electing ship captains and equally dividing their loot. Yet it was "no prey, no pay," so when a likely victim was sighted, the pirate crew usually hoisted a flag of that same country, and then, as the ships sailed close, they raised their freebooters' flag. A flag flown upside-down—internationally recognized as the signal for a ship in distress—was a common pirate trap.

The skull-and-crossbones was flown by Calico Jack Rackham. Born in 1682 and hanged in Jamaica for piracy in 1720, John Rackham received his nickname from the fancy clothes he wore. Calico Jack was famous for hiring two female pirates, Anne Bonny and Mary Read, to join his crew.

To fly your own Jolly Roger, select an actual flag used by historical pirates from the web, trace the flag on page 53, or design your own. Precut stencils are also available from art supply stores.

You'll Need:

- A piece of solid colored cotton or muslin cloth, approximately 36 inches long and 25 inches wide
- Measuring tape
- Scissors
- Straight pins
- Needle
- Thread the same color as the fabric
- Pencil and paper
- Manila folder or card stock
- Masking tape
- Stencil brushes (with blunt ends)
- Fabric paint
- Paper towels
- Several sheets of plain newsprint
- Iron and ironing board
- A dowel
- White glue and brush

Directions

1. Measure the length and width you want your flag to be.
2. Lay the cloth out on a table and mark where you want to cut it. Add ¾ inch at top, bottom, and along one side. Add 1½ inches at the other side if you plan to insert a flagpole. Cut the fabric according to these measurements.
3. Turn under the fabric ¼ inch along three sides. On the side where you want the flagpole, turn it under 1 to 2 inches. Pin the fabric as you go.
4. Stitch the hem in place all the way around. Do the three matching sides first, then the flagpole side, leaving a gap for you to slide the dowel inside.
5. Trace your flag design on a sheet of paper. Cut it out.
6. Use the cutout as a guide to make a stencil from a manila folder or other piece of card stock.
7. Secure the stencil tightly onto the fabric with masking tape so that the paint does not seep underneath.
8. Using a different stencil brush for each color, apply a small amount of fabric paint. Apply the paint from the outside of the stencil toward the center. Keep the brush as dry as possible to avoid leaking or blotting. Dab your brush on a paper towel to remove any excess paint before applying it to the cloth. Use the minimum amount of paint with a light, dotting touch of the brush rather than broad strokes.
9. When the paint is dry, place the flag between sheets of newsprint and use a medium-hot iron to set the design.
10. Brush glue on the length of the dowel that fits into the wide hem. Slide it into the hem and press the fabric to the pole. When the glue is dry, you can attach your Jolly Roger to your bike seat or hang it over your door as a warning to Beware.

Please photocopy or trace this page. Do not cut this book.

Jerk Chicken
for a Buccaneer's Barbecue

Spices are a way of preserving foods that might otherwise spoil quickly in tropical climates. The Taínos, who lived there even before the Arawak and Carib Indians, developed the jerk method of marinating meat or poultry in red hot peppers and spices, then roasting it over a fire built of green allspice or pimento tree branches and leaves, whose wood smoke greatly enhanced the flavor. Pirates learned how to *boucan* (Spanish for "barbecue") from the Arawaks. The word *buccaneers*, another name for these pirates of the Caribbean, comes from this method of cooking outdoors over open fires.

Preparation Time: 15 minutes; marinate 12 hours or overnight
Cooking Time: 30 minutes

Ingredients

2	pounds boneless, skinless chicken pieces, trimmed of fat
3	cloves garlic, chopped
¾	tablespoon ground allspice
½	teaspoon dried thyme
½	teaspoon black pepper
1½	teaspoons ground sage
½	teaspoon ground nutmeg
½	teaspoon ground cinnamon
½	teaspoon salt
2	tablespoons dark brown sugar
¼	cup olive oil
¼	cup Japanese soy sauce
¼	cup white vinegar
½	cup orange juice
	Juice of 1 lime
1	2-inch piece of fresh ginger, grated, or 1 teaspoon powdered ginger
1	green pepper, chopped
½	sweet red pepper, chopped
1	medium onion, chopped
3	scallions or green onions, chopped
1	small Scotch bonnet hot pepper, seeded and chopped (optional)

Make this recipe under adult supervision.

Directions

1. In a large bowl, combine garlic, allspice, thyme, black pepper, sage, nutmeg, cinnamon, salt, and brown sugar. Make a paste of these spices and rub it into the chicken pieces.
2. In a separate bowl, slowly whisk the olive oil, soy sauce, vinegar, orange juice, and lime juice. Then add the ginger, green and red peppers, onions, scallions, and hot pepper (optional). Mix well.
3. Add chicken. Cover and marinate overnight in the refrigerator.
4. Ask **an adult** to prepare and light the outdoor grill. If using charcoal, the grate should be at least 12 inches above the coals.
5. Remove chicken pieces from the marinade, then pour the marinade in a saucepan. Boil the marinade for one minute.
6. Grill the chicken slowly on each side until the chicken is cooked through but still juicy (the juice will be clear). Baste the chicken with the marinade as it grills, turning it often.

This recipe can also be baked in the oven at 375°F for 30 to 50 minutes, depending on the size of the chicken pieces. Baste the chicken with boiled marinade. Cover it with foil if it browns too quickly.

A Bouquet of Tropical Flowers

Huge hibiscus blossoms and poinsettias in scarlet bloom are as common as palm trees in the Caribbean. West Indians, particularly those from Spanish- and French-speaking islands, create colorful paper flowers at home to sell at markets and to tourists debarking from cruise ships.

You'll Need:

- Tissue papers of various colors
- Scissors
- Large chenille stems, preferably green, available at craft stores
- Ribbons of different colors

Directions

1. Cut different-colored tissue paper into different sizes, with the largest about 5 inches across. If you fold the tissue paper sheets lightly in the middle, you can cut a pile of 5 or 6 at a time. Experiment with different shapes, such as hearts, or scallop the edges to look like petals.
2. Place pieces of tissue paper in layers, one color on top of another, in different color patterns. Begin with the largest one on the bottom, building up the pile to the smallest one. You might lay a 12-inch-square of green paper down first to suggest leaves. Make a pile of 12 layers.
3. Poke two holes through the center, about ¾ inch apart.
4. Push a chenille stem up through the hole. Bend the stem and push it down through the other hole. Leave one end long, but twist 2 inches of the other end around the long one. This will create a stem and anchor the sheets of tissue paper together.
5. Ruffle the layers of tissue paper, puffing them out to resemble a flower in bloom.
6. After making a bunch of tropical flowers, tie a ribbon around your bouquet and put it in a vase.

Curried Lamb

Five years after the British parliament abolished slavery in 1833, the practice became illegal in the West Indies. A new source of cheap labor had to be found to work the sugar plantations. Soon, many thousands arrived from India, most as indentured servants under five-year contracts. When their contracts expired, most of them remained as permanent residents, contributing their own cuisine. Trinidad and Tobago, Guyana, and St. Vincent have especially large East Indian populations.

Curry, called *colombo* by the French and *kerry* on the Dutch Islands, supposedly causes a person to sweat, thus cooling the body. Goat meat, a favorite on all the islands, is typical in this recipe, but lamb is easier to obtain in the United States. Served with white rice, coconut flakes, pineapple chunks, and mango chutney on the side, goat curry remains a popular choice for family celebrations.

Preparation Time: 20 minutes
Cooking Time: 30 minutes

Ingredients

1	tablespoon butter
3	tablespoons olive oil
1–2	pounds lean, boneless lamb, trimmed of fat and cut in cubes
1	large onion, chopped
1	green pepper, chopped
½	red pepper, chopped
2	cloves garlic, minced
2	scallions, sliced into ½-inch pieces
3	stalks celery, including celery leaves, chopped
2	tablespoons curry powder

½	teaspoon dried thyme
½	teaspoon turmeric
½	teaspoon basil
½	teaspoon allspice
½	teaspoon cumin
½	teaspoon coriander
¼	cup water
2	potatoes, peeled and cut into cubes
2	tablespoons fresh lime juice
½	cup coconut milk
½	cup chicken broth or stock

Salt and pepper to taste

Make this recipe under adult supervision.

Directions

1. Melt the butter in the oil. Drop in the lamb cubes and brown them on all sides.
2. Add onions, green and red peppers, garlic, scallions, and celery. Sauté until soft.
3. In a bowl, mix the curry powder, thyme, turmeric, basil, allspice, cumin, and coriander. Add the water to make curry paste.
4. Add the potato cubes to the lamb and vegetables simmering on the stove.
5. Mix the curry paste, lime juice, coconut milk, chicken broth, and salt and pepper to taste. Add this to the lamb and vegetables. Cover and simmer on low another hour, stirring several times.

Further Reading

Books

Bastyra, Judy. *Living in Jamaica.* London: Franklin Watts, Ltd., 2005, 2007.

Blashfield, Jean F. *Haiti.* New York: Scholastic/Children's Press, 2007.

Browlie, Ali, and Susan M. Cunningham. *Jamaica.* United Kingdom and Jamaica: Bojang & Cunningham, 2006.

Hernandez, Romel. *Caribbean Islands: Facts and Figures.* Broomall, PA: Mason Crest Publishers, 2008.

Kozleski, Lisa. *The Leeward Islands.* Broomall, PA: Mason Crest Publishers, 2009.

Miller, Debra A. *Jamaica.* San Diego, CA: Lucent Publishers, 2006.

Pohl, Kathleen. *Looking at Cuba.* Milwaukee: Gareth Stevens Publisher, 2008.

Rogers, Lura, and Barbara Radcliffe-Rogers. *The Dominican Republic.* New York: Scholastic/Children's Press, 2008.

Torres, John. *Meet Our New Student from Haiti.* Hockessin, DE: Mitchell Lane Publishers, 2008.

Weintraub, Aileen. *Anne Bonny and Mary Read: Fearsome Female Pirates of the Eighteenth Century.* New York: Rosen, 2005.

Works Consulted

Carter, E. H., G. W. Digby, and R. N. Murray. *The Story of Our Islands: History of the West Indian Peoples.* London, England & Ontario, Canada: Thomas Nelson & Sons, Ltd., 1964, 1980.

DeMers, John. *Caribbean Cooking.* New York: Penguin Putnam, Inc., 1989, 1997.

Ferguson, James. *A Traveller's History of the Caribbean.* New York: Interlink, 1999.

Harris, Dunstan. *Island Cooking: Recipes from the Caribbean.* St. Thomas, Virgin Islands: Crossing Press, 1990; Ten Speed Press, 2003.

Higman, B. W. *Jamaican Food: History, Biology, Culture.* Kingston: University of West Indies Press, 2008.

Johnson, Captain Charles. *A General History of the Robberies & Murders of the Most Notorious Pirates.* London, 1724; reprint: New York: The Lyons Press & Conway Maritime Press, 1998.

Kaufman, Cheryl Davidson. *Cooking the Caribbean Way.* Minneapolis, MN: Lerner Publications, 1988, 2002.

Konstam, Angus. *The History of Pirates.* In Association with The Mariners' Museum, Virginia. Guilford, CT: The Pequot Press & The Lyons Press, 2002.

Lalbachan, Pamela. *The Complete Caribbean Cook Book.* Boston; Rutland, VT; Tokyo: Charles E. Tuttle Co., Inc., 1998.

Morgan, Jinx and Jefferson. *The Sugar Mill Caribbean Cookbook: Casual & Elegant Recipes Inspired by the Islands.* Boston: Harvard Common Press, 1996.

Further Reading

Spence, Wenton O. *Jamaican Cookery: Recipes from Old Jamaican Grandmothers.* Kingston, Jamaica: Heritage Publishers, 2004.

Springer, Rita G. *Caribbean Cookbook: A Lifetime of Recipes.* Jamaica: Ian Randle, 2000.

Willinsky, Helen. *Jerk from Jamaica: Barbecue Caribbean Style.* Berkeley, CA: Ten Speed Press, 2007.

Wolfe, Linda, and the Editors of Time-Life Books. *The Cooking of the Caribbean Islands.* New York: Time-Life, 1970.

Woodard, Colin. *The Republic of Pirates.* New York: Harcourt, 2007.

On the Internet

Caribbean Choice
http://www.caribbeanchoice.com/

Caribbean Culture
http://caribbean-guide.info/past.and.present/culture/

Caribbean Tourism Organization
http://www.doitcaribbean.com

Coloring: Seashells by Millhill
http://seashellsbymillhill.wordpress.com/coloring-pages/

Curaçao
http://www.curacao-tourism.com

History of Barbados
http://http://www.barbados.org/history1.htm

Jamaica Culture, Map, Flag, Tourist Places
http://www.sphereinfo.com/jamaica-history-culture-religion.htm

Martinique
http://www.martinique.org/

Republic of Pirates: Calico Jack Rackham
http://republicofpirates.net/Rackham.html

Sailors' Valentine Lore
http://www.sailors-valentine.com/sailors_valentine_lore.html

St. Kitts
http://www.stkitts-tourism.com

St. Vincent & the Grenadines
http://www.svgtourism.com

U.S. Virgin Islands
http://www.usvitourism.vi/

Glossary

Barbado (bar-BAY-doh)—To exile a debtor, petty criminal, or political foe to the Caribbean Islands, especially Barbados, in order to serve out a legal sentence by laboring in the sugarcane fields.

barbecue (BAR-beh-kyoo)—The method of cooking meat or poultry with sauces or spices outside over an open fire.

boil (BOYL)—To heat a liquid on a stove until it bubbles.

broil (BROYL)—To cook food, such as meat or poultry, under direct heat.

buccaneers (buh-kuh-NEERS)—Pirates or sea robbers who raided Spanish coasts, the West Indies, and other areas throughout the seventeenth through early nineteenth centuries. Their name comes from their favored method of grilling meat outside over open fires.

cay (KAY)—A low-lying island, coral reef, or sandbar that is separated from the mainland.

chutney (CHUT-nee)—A relish, originally from East India, that is made from fruits, particularly mangoes or peaches, and cooked with raisins, herbs, various spices, and lemon juice or vinegar, and served with meat, especially lamb and goat.

conquistadores (kun-kee-stuh-DOOR-eez)—From the Spanish word meaning "conquerors," Spanish soldiers who militarily overcame then occupied Mexico, Peru, and what is now the West Indies.

indigenous (in-DIH-juh-nus)—Belonging to a particular place; the original people of a region and a native of that place.

jumbie (JUM-bee)—The West Indian word for "zombie," a ghost or member of the walking dead, and one that is at the basis of much Caribbean folklore.

marinate (MAYR-ih-nayt)—To soak meat or other ingredients in a sauce for a period of time before it is cooked.

privateers (pry-vah-TEERS)—Privately owned ships and their crews commissioned by a government during wartime to attack and capture enemy military and merchant ships.

rice table—An Indonesian meal popular in the Dutch West Indies, at which at least twenty different dishes are offered at the same time.

sauté (saw-TAY)—To brown meat or vegetables in a small amount of butter or oil in a pan on top of the stove.

scallop (SKAL-up)—A series of curves or segments of circles forming a decorative edge on paper or cloth.

soursop (SOUR-sop)—A sweet fruit with many seeds that grows abundantly on trees throughout the West Indies and can be eaten fresh or used to make juice, sherbets, or tropical drinks.

tsunami (soo-NAH-mee)—A tidal wave caused by some great disturbance beneath the ocean, such as an earthquake or volcanic eruption.

zooxanthellae (zoo-oh-ZAN-thuh-lee)—Microscopic animals that live within the cells of coral polyps, the animals that build coral reefs.

Index

Africa/Africans 6, 9, 14, 16, 28, 32, 36
Antilles, Greater and Lesser 4
Arawak Indians 4–5, 9, 54
Aruba 4, 6
bananas 9, 48–49
Barbados 5, 6, 32, 44, 46
Bligh, Captain William 9
Bonaire 5, 6
Brazil 6, 32
British 6, 8, 26, 28, 29, 34, 50, 58
buccaneers 50, 54
cacao 9, 34
calabash 14, 22
calypso 28, 30, 36
Carib Indians 4, 5, 32, 34, 54
Carnival 28, 36, 38–39
Christmas 26, 28, 29
coconut(s) 9, 11, 12, 26–27, 58
Columbus, Christopher 4, 5, 34
conquistadores 5
Cuba/Cubans 4, 5, 8, 24
Curacao 5, 6
Denmark 7
Dominica 4, 5, 7, 32
Dominican Republic 4, 5, 8, 24
Dutch 5, 6, 9, 16, 50, 58
earthquakes 6
England/English 5, 6, 34, 50
Europe/Europeans 5, 6, 40, 48, 50
flying fish 44
France/French 5, 6, 7, 34, 40, 50, 56, 58
Greaves, Redlegs 6
Grenada 5, 34
Guadeloupe 5, 6, 16
Guyana 58
Haiti 4, 5, 6, 20
hurricanes 6
India 4, 9, 58
Jamaica 5, 6, 9, 16, 32, 40, 50, 51
Leeward Islands 4
L' Ouverture, Toussaint 6

Martinique 4, 5, 6, 16
Montserrat 5, 7
musical instruments
 guiros 28, 29
 maracas 28, 29
 steel drums 28, 30–31, 36
Nevis 6
pirate (s) 6, 50–52, 54
plantain(s) 8, 9, 28
Portugal 6
Powell, Captain John 6
Puerto Rico 4, 8, 24, 36
Rackham, John (Calico Jack) 51
Saba 5, 7
St. Christopher (St. Kitts) 5, 6
St. Eustatius (Statia) 5, 7
St. Lucia 5, 6
St. Maarten/St. Martine 5, 6
St. Pierre (Martinique) 5, 6
St. Vincent 4, 5, 9, 16, 32, 58
shells 7, 18–19, 22, 46–47
slavery 6, 9, 14, 32, 40, 50, 58
Soufrière, Mount 5
Spain/Spanish 5, 6, 24, 28, 50
Spanish-speaking islands 8, 28, 29, 41, 56
spices 9, 32, 34–35, 48, 54
Stamp and Go 40–41
sugar industry 6, 9, 32, 40, 50, 58
Suriname 7
Taíno Indians 4, 28, 54
Three Kings' Day 28
Tortuga 50
Trinidad and Tobago 4, 5, 16, 30, 50, 58
United States 6, 7, 8, 24, 40, 48, 58
U.S. Virgin Islands 4, 7
Venezuela 4, 5, 6
volcanic eruptions 5, 6
Windward Islands 4

PHOTO CREDITS: Cover, pp. 1, 2–3, 4–5, 7, 12, 15, 16, 18–19, 20–21, 23, 28, 30, 31, 37, 39, 44, 48, 50, 51, 53, 56—Creative Commons; p. 29—John Miles; all other photos—Juliet Mofford. Every effort has been made to locate all copyright holders of material used in this book. If any errors or omissions have occurred, corrections will be made in future editions of the book.

Juliet Haines Mofford and her husband taught in a boys' boarding school outside San Juan, where most of their students were native Puerto Ricans or from the U.S. Virgin Islands. With their two small children, they celebrated Three Kings' Day with jibaro families in the island's remote mountains.

The Moffords sailed and camped throughout the Virgin Islands, spent several months doing historical research on Barbados, and lived for a year on St. Vincent, where the author's father-in-law was born and many relatives remain, including some who appeared in the *Pirates of the Caribbean* movies. During months of historical research in Barbados, they even discovered a real pirate named Redlegs Greaves in their family tree! Mofford has written about the West Indies for the *New York Times, Boston Globe, Chicago Tribune, Montreal Gazette,* and magazines such as *Caribbean Beachcomber* and *Tropic.* She and her husband have traded the tropics for a landlubber's life in New England.